# Is it flexible or rigid?

## Sheila Fletcher

**Crabtree Publishing Company**

www.crabtreebooks.com

# What's the Matter?

**Author:** Sheila Fletcher
**Publishing plan research and development:**
  Sean Charlebois, Reagan Miller
  Crabtree Publishing Company
**Project development:** Clarity Content Services
**Project management:** Karen Iversen
**Project coordinator:** Kathy Middleton
**Editors:** Sheila Fletcher, Kathy Middleton
**Copy editor:** Dimitra Chronopoulos
**Proofreader:** Reagan Miller
**Design:** First Image
**Photo research:** Linda Tanaka
**Prepress technician:** Katherine Berti
**Print and production coordinator:** Katherine Berti

**Photographs:**
p1 m.bonotto/shutterstock; p4 Monkey Business Images/shutterstock; p5 left clockwise George.M./shutterstock, John Kasawa/dreamstime.com, Africa Studio/shutterstock; p6 Balazs Justin/shutterstock; p7 top left clockwise Swissmacky/shutterstock, Gelpi/shutterstock, scattoselvaggio/shutterstock, john a. shaw/shutterstock; p8 iStockphoto/Thinkstock; p9 clockwise Aaron Amat/shutterstock; iStockphoto/Thinkstock; Polka Dot Images/Thinkstock; p10 top Szefei/shutterstock, 55hasan/dreamstime.com; p11 Daseaford/shutterstock; p12 HomeStudio/shutterstock; p13 Orange Line Media/shutterstock; p14 left Brian Guest/shutterstock, prochasson frederic/shutterstock; p15 left Brandon Bourdages/shutterstock; iStockphoto/Thinkstock, Hemera/Thinkstock; p17 left Peter S/shutterstock, topseller/shutterstock; p19 Pierdelune/dreamstime.com; p20 Quayside/shutterstock; p21 Jacetan/dreamstime.com; p22 left Stockbyte/Thinkstock, iStockphoto/Thinkstock; cover shutterstock

**Library and Archives Canada Cataloguing in Publication**

Fletcher, Sheila, 1943-
    Is it flexible or rigid? / Sheila Fletcher.

(What's the matter?)
Includes index.
Issued also in electronic formats.
ISBN 978-0-7787-2047-8 (bound).--ISBN 978-0-7787-2054-6 (pbk.)

    1. Flexure--Juvenile literature.  2. Matter--Properties--Juvenile literature.  I. Title.  II. Series: What's the matter? (St. Catharines, Ont.)

TA417.7.F5F54 2012        j620.1'123        C2012-900289-5

**Library of Congress Cataloging-in-Publication Data**

Fletcher, Sheila, 1943-
Is it flexible or rigid? / Sheila Fletcher.
p. cm. -- (What's the matter?)
Includes index.
ISBN 978-0-7787-2047-8 (reinforced library binding : alk. paper) --
ISBN 978-0-7787-2054-6 (pbk. : alk. paper) -- ISBN 978-1-4271-7945-6 (electronic pdf) -- ISBN 978-1-4271-8060-5 (electronic html)
1. Matter--Properties--Juvenile literature. 2. Elasticity--Juvenile literature. 3. Hardness--Juvenile literature. I. Title.

QC173.36.F54 2012
531'.382--dc23
                    2012000117

# Crabtree Publishing Company

www.crabtreebooks.com        1-800-387-7650

Printed in the U.S.A./032012/CJ20120215

**Published in Canada**
**Crabtree Publishing**
616 Welland Ave.
St. Catharines, ON
L2M 5V6

**Published in the United States**
**Crabtree Publishing**
PMB 59051
350 Fifth Avenue, 59th Floor
New York, New York 10118

**Published in the United Kingdom**
**Crabtree Publishing**
Maritime House
Basin Road North, Hove
BN41 1WR

**Published in Australia**
**Crabtree Publishing**
3 Charles Street
Coburg North
VIC 3058

# What is in this book?

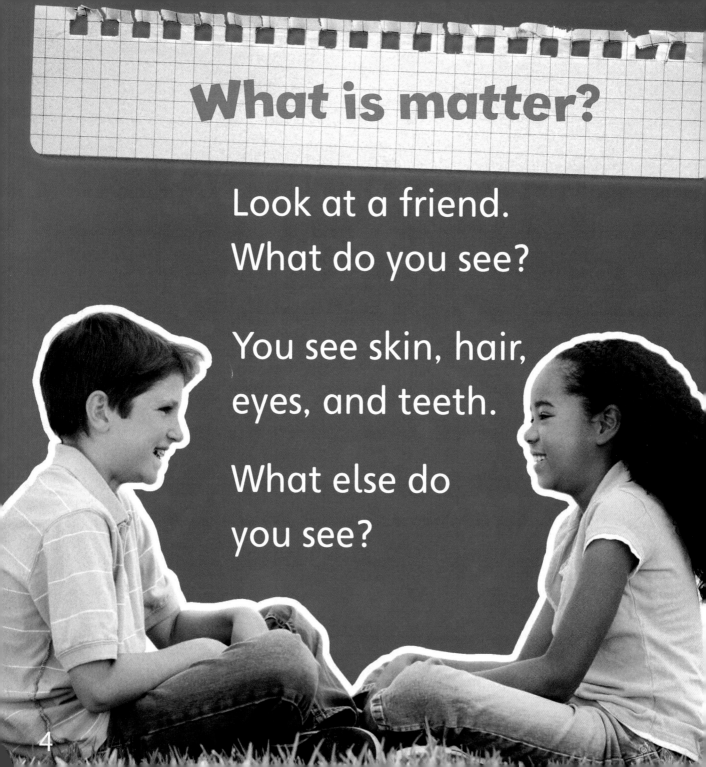

# What is matter?

Look at a friend.
What do you see?

You see skin, hair,
eyes, and teeth.

What else do
you see?

4

All of these different things are the same in one way.

All things are made of **matter**.

Matter is anything that takes up space and has **mass**, such as a shoe, a desk, a chair, or socks.

Mass is the amount of material in an object.

# Properties

Different kinds of matter have different **properties**.

Properties describe how something looks, feels, tastes, smells, or sounds.

For example, hard and soft are properties that describe how something feels.

6

Sweet and sour are properties that describe how something tastes.

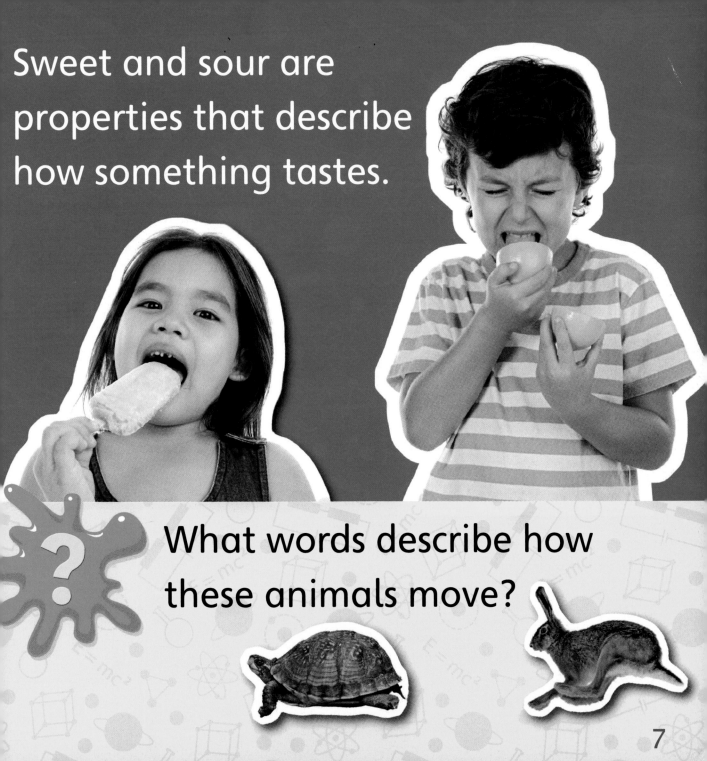

What words describe how these animals move?

# Is it flexible?

Some things can bend.

Another word we can use is **flexible**.

Flexible things can bend easily and not break.

The word flexible describes a property of matter.

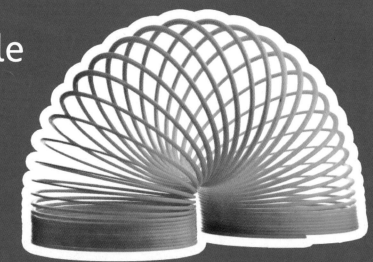

# These things are flexible.

garbage
bag

hair
elastics

trampoline

# Flexible things

Look at the objects on this page.

Each of these objects has a flexible hose.

How does a flexible hose help when you are washing a car or vacuuming a room?

Why does this spider web not break when the wind blows it?

# It does not bend.

Sometimes, we use materials that are not flexible.

They do not bend.

They are stiff. Another word we can use is **rigid**.

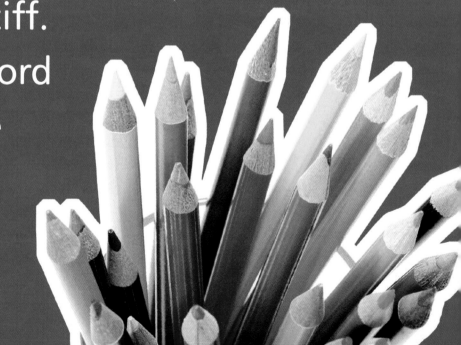

What would happen if you tried to hang on monkey bars that were not rigid?

13

# Flexible or rigid?

Which of these materials are flexible? Which one is rigid?

Would a flag made of metal or a baseball bat made of licorice work very well? Why or why not?

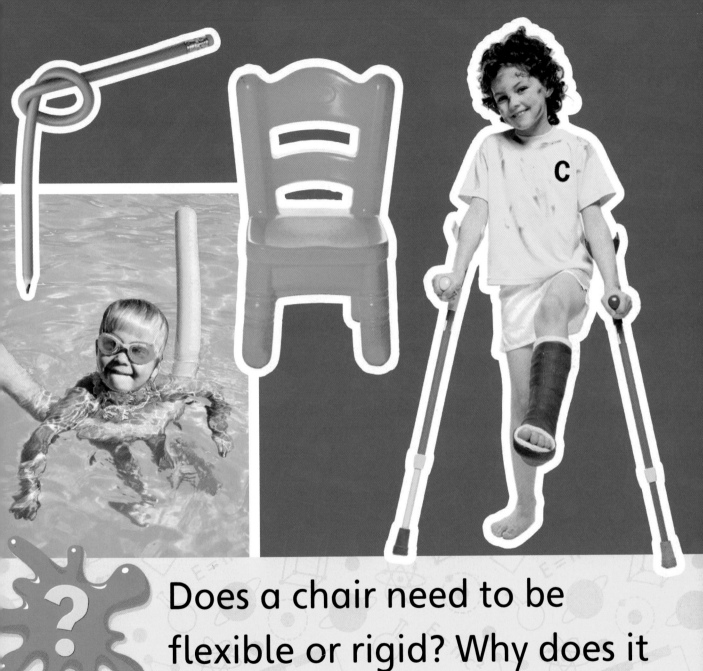

Does a chair need to be flexible or rigid? Why does it need to have that property?

# Not quite rigid

Cooked noodles are flexible and can bend.

Noodles that are not cooked are rigid and will break if you bend them.

Rigid objects that are big can also break Bridges and buildings are tall and rigid. But they must also be a bit flexible or strong winds could knock them down.

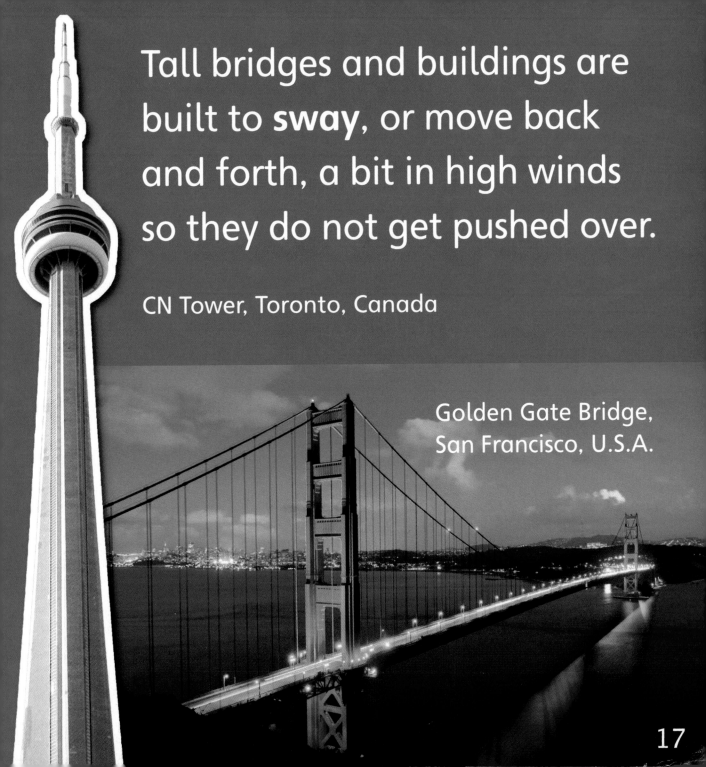

Tall bridges and buildings are built to **sway**, or move back and forth, a bit in high winds so they do not get pushed over.

CN Tower, Toronto, Canada

Golden Gate Bridge, San Francisco, U.S.A.

# Can they change?

We can change some rigid materials to make them flexible.

People made the first snowshoes out of wood.

They soaked the wood in water to make it flexible.

Then they bent the wood into the shape they needed.

# Make it!

Find some straws that are flexible.

Find some straws that are rigid.

Try to build some shapes, a building, or even people by connecting the straws together.

Which kind of straw would you use to make corners?

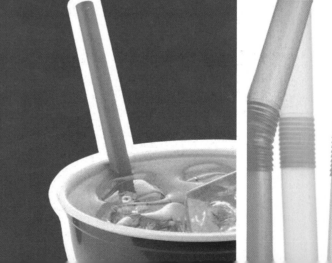

Which kind of straw would you use to make a tall tower?

21

# Flexible you!

Which parts of your body help you stand up straight?

Which parts of your body help you curl up into a ball?

Which body part in your back can be either rigid or flexible?

22

# Words to know and Index

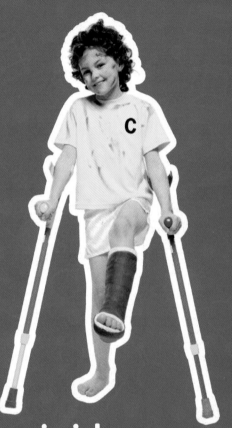

# Notes for adults

## Objectives
- to introduce children to the concept of properties of matter
- to introduce children to the properties of flexibility and rigidity
- to help children observe and understand how we use flexible and rigid objects

## Prerequisite
Have the children read other books in this series, such as *Is it hot or cold?*, *Is it smooth or rough?*, or *Is it heavy or light?* These books discuss properties of matter with which children will be familiar.

## Questions before reading *Is it flexible or rigid?*
"What would it be like if you couldn't bend at the waist? How would you pick up anything you dropped on the floor?"

"If the bones in your legs were made of rubber, what do you think would happen when you tried to stand up?"

"Show me something in the room that can bend. How would you use it?"

"Show me something in the room that is rigid. How would you use it?"

## Discussion
Read the book to the children or share the reading with them. Have the children say the words properties, flexible, and rigid. You may wish to encourage the children to contribute to a list of flexible and rigid items. Post the list in a prominent place, and discuss items as children suggest them. For each suggestion, ask the children why the object needs to be flexible or rigid.

For the straw construction activity on pages 20-21, have the children twist the end of a straw in order to insert it into another straw.

## Extension
Tell the children about Joseph B. Friedman, who watched his little girl drink soda pop with a straw that didn't bend. She had trouble reaching the straw.
As a result of that experience, he invented flexible straws. Encourage the children to tell you about items in their own experience that they wish would (or wouldn't) bend.